Merino wool: Derived from a speci
it is the softest of all wools. The fibe
heat retention, is durable and does n
discomfort.

Len Merino
Wool from Merino sheep

Alpaca wool: South American camel family. This coat is as soft as Cashmere and lighter than regular fleece. Alpaca fur retains heat well, is soft and durable.

Alpaca wool
Wool from Alpaca camels

3. What to prepare when crocheting?

Tools: Find and buy wool & crochet needles/knitting needles at the market, stationery stores or handmade shops.

Choose a wool that is not ruffled (e.g. cotton milk) & is just the right size. As for the crochet needle/knitting rod, choose the type that fits the yarn size so that when the hook does not slip off.

Choose popular products with basic stitches to practice. Usually knitting will be a shawl and crocheting will be a hat.

You can find the easiest ways to crochet a scarf, or tutorials on how to crochet a beanie, ... in knitting forums.

Learn & learn basic stitches (Knitting: Up stitch, down stitch, round stitch, ... Crochet: Single stitch, double stitch, pin stitch, ...).

There are many knitting tutorials online as well as knitting books from the most basic.

Once you have mastered the basic stitches, you can go online to find charts & tutorials on high skills to create more sophisticated & patterned products.
Learn about product color schemes for eye-catching harmony.

Practice using more advanced tools if needed.

CONTENTS

Bottle Hat Hook

Materials to prepare:

- Wool yarn: Woven yarn or raw yarn
- Color: main blue, a little dark blue, a little black and a little white
- Needle hook: 2.5mm – 3.0mm
- Accessories: woolen scissors, woolen needle, marker

Abbreviated symbols:

MR: Magic circle
X: Single crochet stitch
V: Increase stitch (2 single sts hooked to 1 leg)
A: Reduce stitch (2 single crochet stitches)
B: Sprocket/chain stitch
T: Semi-double stitch
VT: Semi-double stitches (2 semi-double stitches hooked to 1 leg)

Bottle cap (blue)

H1: MR, 10T

H2: 10VT

H3: (1T, 1VT)*10

H4: (1T, 2VT)*10

H5: (3T, 1VT)*10

H6: (2T, 1VT), (4T, 1VT)*9, 2T

H7: 60TILLION

H8: (5T, 1VT)*10

H9: (3T, 1VT), (6T, 1VT)*9, 3T

H10: (7T, 1VT)*10

H11: 90T

H12: (4T, 1VT), (8T, 1VT)*9, 4T

H13: 100TILLION

H14: (8T,1VT)*10

H15–H26: 110T, 2X, remove 1 foot to make 1 stitch to move the end of the bottle cap.

II. Hat brim (blue)

H1: 1B, (3X, 1V)*9, 3X

H2: 1B, return, 1A, 44X, 1A

H3: 1B, return, 1A, 42X, 1A

H4: 1B, return, 1A, 40X, 1A

H5: 1B, return, 1A, 38X, 1A

H6: 1B, back, 1A, 4X, (1V, 6X)*4, 1V, 3X, 1A

H7: 1B, return, 1A, 39X, 1A

H8: 1B, return, 1A, 37X, 1A

H9: 1B, return, 1A, 35X, 1A

H10: 1B, return, 1A, 4X, 1A, 21X, 1A, 4X, 1A

H11: 1B, return, 1A, 29X, 1A

H12: 1B, return, 1A, 4X, 1A, 15X, 1A, 4X, 1A

H13: 1B, return, 1A, 23X, 1A

1B, thread trimming

III. The yellow rim of the hat begins at the corner of the hat body and brim (dark green).

H1: (1X, 1V)*8, 17X, (1V, 1X)*8 move the nose to the body of the hat, add 1 more to the side and then 1B back.

H2: each foot hook 1X, then move the nose to the body of the hat, add 1 more stitch to the side and then 1B back.

H3: Each 1X crochet leg goes to the end of the row and then moves the nose to the end of the hat body (Note that you should crochet a single stitch in row 3 to wrap the single stitch of H2 for the rim to create a ribbed shape as a highlight for the rim)

Sheep Keychain

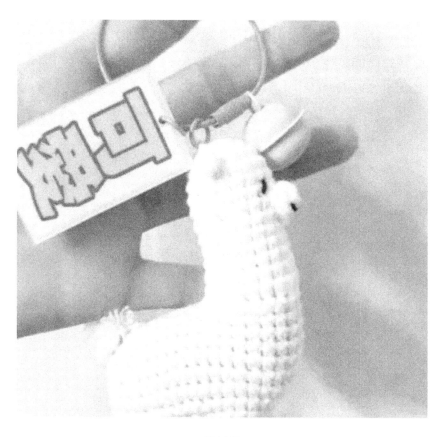

Materials to prepare:

- Yarn: Wool Jeans Yarn Art Turkey
- Color: 2.5mm . hook
- Needle hook: 2.5mm
- Accessories: Cotton, sewing needles, scissors, keychains

Abbreviated symbols:

X: single stitch
V: increase nose
A: nose reduction
T: semi-double stitch
M: 3 single stitches with 1 hook foot

Making:
I, Head, Body and Legs
Row 1. MR6X
Row 2. 6V

Row 3. XV*6 = 18

Rows 4 to 11. 18X

Row 12. 8X, 2T, 8X

Row 13. 7X, 4T, 7X

Row 14.8

Row 15. V, 6X, 18X, 6X, VUC

Row 16. 2V, 30X, 2V

Row 17. XV*2, 30X, XV*2

Row 18. 2XV*2, 30X, 2XV*2

Rows 19- 23. 46X

Row 24. X, 5XA*3, 2X, 5XV*3, X

Row 25. X, 4 pins, skip 6 hooks, 6X, 4 pins, skip 6 hooks, 2X, 4 pins, skip 6 hooks, 6X, 4 pins, skip 6 hooks, X

Row 26. X, 2A, X, M, (2X, 2A)*2, X, M, 2X, 2A, X

Row 27. 10X

Row 28.5A

II, Muzzle

Row 1. MR, 10X

Row 2. 10X
Row 3. 5A
III, Ears (2)
Row 1. 6X
Row 2. 2X, V, 2X, DRAW
IV, Nose
4 spinning wheels: T, T, X

Finishing products:
Sew the parts together

Gile Knitting Chart

Materials to prepare:

Wool yarn: Alize lana gold
Color:
Needle hook: number 4.0mm

Accessories: wool sewing needles, wool cutting scissors, ...

Sign:

MR: magic circle
X: single stitch
V: increase the nose (2 stitches on 1 leg)
A: reduce the stitches (2 stitches together)

Making:

How to knit:

The whole shirt is nose down or up

Right side knit (knit down)

Rib knit 1 reverse side (knit up)

Can knit 3 pieces or knit 1 piece (like the author)
The size of the shirt I knit is 13-15kg, 85-95cm high

Catch the nose:

2 front flaps 32 stitches each

The bra has 6 stitches, so the back body is calculated:
32 + 32 − 6 = 58 stitches

Knit 1 piece, total: 58 + 32 + 32 = 122 stitches

If knitting 3 pieces, add 1 stitch for each flap to sew.
Back body add 2 stitches 1 on each side for stitching

12 stitches knit

Buttons: every 15 ways to create buttons 1 time
Knit the shirt button up, the hem knit 2 up 2 down
Fully knit on the body, 6 stitches after 6 stitches, the
right side rib is knit up, the right side is down

After 6 rows on the body, go to the owl, the right
side is knitting down, the left side is knitting up.
According to the following chart:

1. 12K CZK
2. 12P
3. 3 sts wait for 3K knitting, 3K knitting wait 3 sts
out and wait for 3K knitting, 3K knitting
4-16: plain knitting (K right side, P left side)
17. 3 sts wait to go back, krl 2K, knit 2K wait, wait
for 1K to wait for the left hand needle to continue
knitting K2tog.

Take 3 sts on the stick and wait to come out first, return the first stitch to the left hand knit K2tog with the first stitch of 3K on the stick, knit the remaining 2K and continue knitting the 2K wait, Kll

18. 10P
19–24. plain knitting
25. 3 stitches out of the waiting rod, 2K . for the back to knit
Knit 3P on the waiting stick
2 sts on the waiting stick, put 3P . in front
Knitting 2K sticks
Knit up to 25cm, then cut the armpit
symbol: W + T knit short lines
Lap 1 knit the neck to the armpit (right side)
1. 6K, W + T, 6K
2. 6K, P, 19K, P, 5K
3. 5K, W + T, 5K
4. 5K, K2TOG, 18K, 1K, 6K

5. 6K, P2TOG, 16K, P2TOG, 5K

6. 5K, K2TOG, 15K, 1K, 6K

7. 6K, P2TOG, 13K, P2TOG, 5K

8. 5K, 1K, 13K, 1K, 6K

9. 6K, P2TOG, 11K, P2TOG, 5K

10. 5K, 1K, 11K, 1K, 6K

11. 6K, P2TOG, 9K, P2TOG, 5K

12. 5K, 1K, 9K, 1K, 6K

13. 6K, P2TOG, 7K, P2TOG, 5K

14.5K, 1K, 7K, 1K, 6K

15. 6K, P2TOG, 6K, 1P, 5K

16.5K, 1K, 6K, 1K, 6K

17. 6K, P2TOG, 5K, 1P, 5K

18.5K, 1K, 5K, 1K, 6K

19. 6K, P2TOG, 4K, 1P, 5K

20. 5K, 1K, 4K, 1K, 6

21. 6K, P2TOG, 3K, 1P, 5K

22.5K, 1K, 3K, 1K, 6K

23-42. Smooth knitting. Chic (knitted rhyme as below)

Knit 2. From armpit to neck

1. 5K, W + T, 5K
2. 5K, 1P, 19K, 1P, 6K
3. 6K, W + T, 6K
4. 6K, 1K, 18K, K2TOG, 5K
5. 5K, P2TOG, 16K, P2TOG, 6K
6. 6K, 1K, 15K, K2TOG, 5K
7. 5K, P2TOG, 13K, P2TOG, 6K
8. 6K, 1K, 13K, 1K, 5K
9. 5K, P2TOG, 11K, P2TOG, 6K
10. 6K, 1K, 11K, 1K, 5K
11. 5K, P2TOG, 9K, P2TOG, 6K
12. 6K, 1K, 9K, 1K, 5K
1. 5K, P2TOG, 7K, P2TOG, 6K
14. 6K, 1K, 7K, 1K, 5K
15. 5K, 1P, 6K, P2TOG, 6K
16. 6K, 1K, 6K, 1K, 5K
17. 5K, 1P, 5K, P2TOG, 6K
18. 6K, 1K, 5K, 1K, 5K
19. 5K, 1P, 4K, P2TOG, 6K
20. 6K, 1K, 4K, 1K, 5K
21. 5K, 1P, 3K, P2TOG, 6K

22. 6K, 1K, 4K, 1K, 5K

23-42. Smooth knit with splints. Extraction

Back knit. Obverse

1. 5K, W + T, 5K

2. 5K, 1P, 46K, 1P, 5K

3. 5K, W + T, 5K

4. 5K, K2TOG, 44K, K2TOG, 5K CZK

5. 5K, P2TOG, 42K, P2TOG, 5K

6. 5K, K2TOG, 40K, K2TOG, 5K CZK

7. 5K, P2TOG, 38K, P2TOG, 5K

8. Entire stitch

9. 5K, P2TOG, 36K, P2TOG, 5K

10. Entire stitch

11. 5K, P2TOG, 34K, P2TOG, 5K

12. Entire stitch

1. 5K, P2TOG, 32K, P2TOG, 5K

14. Entire stitch

15-34. Smooth knitting with splints

35. 16K, W + T, 16K, W + T, 16K, W + T, 16K, knit up 10 rows with 16K ribbed to row 45 start extracting 16 skinny sts add 5 more sts back to the left needle and then extract next, those 5 and 26 more

16 sts left on left needle, knit 10 more rows with 16 sts left and then extract

Sewing clothes. Complete

Mandala Coaster Hooks

Materials to prepare:

- Yarn: Turkish YarnArt Jeans Wool
- Color: brown, blue, dark pink, gray and light pink
- Hook Needle: 4mm
- Accessories: Scissors, wool sewing needles.

Abbreviated symbols:

MR: magic circle
X: single stitch
F: single double stitch
X: single crochet stitch
Sl st: slip tip

Making:

Using the F . tip
R1: Brown wool: MR, 3 pins, 11F. Slst on first double nose pin = [12F

R2: 3 pins (counted as 1 F), 1F, (2F with the same foot) to the end of the row. Slst into the first double nose pin = [24F]

R3: 3 pins (counts as 1 F stitch), 1F, (FV, F)* repeat all the way = [36F]

R4: Swap blue wool, {(1F, 1 pin, 1F) on the same leg, skip 1 st F} * repeat all the way. Slst into the base of the first double stitch= [36F, 18 spaces equals 1 pitch]
R5: Change to dark pink wool. (5F in the space of 1 stitch in row 4, 2 in)* repeat all the way through. [18 clusters of 5F, 18 gaps of 2 pins]

R6: Change the gray wool. (4X into the 2-point gap, 1 X into the center of the 5F cluster)* repeat all the way. Slst to the foot of the first X nose = [90X]

R7: Change to light pink wool. (1X, 1F, 1X) on the same hook foot, skipping 2 X sts)* repeat all the way = [60X, 30F]

Fasten yarn, cut wool

Tutorial on how to crochet Mandala Coasterl by Oombawka Design Crochet

Finishing products:

Use a sewing needle to hide excess wool inside the product.

Crochet Bear Cup Decoration

Materials to prepare:

- Yarn: Turkish YarnArt Jeans Wool
- Color: yellow, brown, red, white, pink
- Needle hook: 2.5mm

Accessories: Cotton wool, scissors, woolen sewing needles, animal eyes, white felt fabric

Abbreviated symbols:

MR: magic circle
X: single stitch
V: increase nose
A: nose reduction

Making:
I, Cup body
Brown wool
54 pins, round

Rows 1–2. 1 pin, 54X, sl = 54

Row 3. 1 pin, (7X,A)*6 , sl = 48

Red color change

Rows 4–5. 1 pin, 48X, sl = 48

Yellow change

Row 6. 1 pin, BLO– 48X, sl = 48

Rows 7–11. 1 pin, 48X, sl = 48

Yarn dowel

II, Ear (2)

Row 1. MR, 6X = 6

Row 2. 6V = 12

Row 3.(X,V)*6 = 18

Rows 4–6. 18X

Fasten the yarn, leaving a long piece of yarn for sewing

III, Nose

4 pins, rotating hook on leg 2:

Row 1. 2X, W, X, V= 8

Row 2. (V,X)*4 = 12

Row 3. (V, 3X, V, X)*2 = 16

Fasten the yarn, leaving a long piece of yarn for sewing

IV, Towel

Use red wool to crochet on the 6th row

Row 1. 5X, spin

Rows 2-4. 5X, rotate

Row 5. V, sl, V, sl, V

Yarn dowel

Finishing products:

+ Sewing 2 ears

+ Stitch the nose

+ Attach plastic eyes

+ Cut a piece of white felt cloth and stick it in front of the ear, cut the pink felt fabric for the cheeks, cut a heart shape and stick it on the ear

+ Use brown embroidery thread to embroider bear nose.

Rainbow Music Cushion Hook

Materials to prepare:

- Yarn: Wool Jeans Yarn Art Turkey
- Color: gray, brown, light yellow, beige, white, gray
- Needle hook: 2.5mm

Accessories: Cotton, woolen needle, scissors, marker

Abbreviated symbols:

X: single stitch
V: increase nose
A: nose reduction
Sl: slip nose

Making:
I, Rainbow (depending on color arrangement)
Color 1

Row 1. 24 pins

Row 2. Hook on 2 pins, return to hook on 3rd leg: 24T, 2 spinning pins = 24

Row 3. 8T, (1T, 1TV)*4, 8T, 2 reels = 28

Color 2

Row 4. 10T, 8TV, 10T, 2 reels = 36

Row 5. 36T, 2 reels

Color 3

Row 6. 13T, 10TV, 13T, 2 reels = 46

Row 7. 46T, 2 cranks

Color 4

Row 8. 14T, (2T, 1TV)*6, 14T, 2 reels = 52

Row 9. 12T, (3T, 1TV)*7, 12T, 2 reels = 59

Color 5

Row 10. 59T, 2 cranks

Row 11. 15T, 1TV, (3T, 1TV)*7, 15T, 1 wheel = 67

Color 6

Row 12. 66X, 1V, make the bottom border of the rainbow with 36X

II, Music box zipper

Prepare the music box before starting

Remove the end of the zipper and replace it with a teardrop wool pad (see picture).

Row 1. MR, 6X = 6

Row 2. 6V = 12

Row 3. (X,V)*6 = 18

Row 4. (2X,V)*6 = 24

Rows 5-7. 24X

Row 8. (2X, A)*6 = 18

Rows 9-10. 18X

Row 11. (X,A)*6= 12

Row 12. 12X

Row 13. 6A= 6

Yarn cutting pins

Finishing products:

Kitty Cat Key Chain Pattern

Materials to prepare:

- Yarn: Wool Jeans Yarn Art Turkey
- Color: white, pink, blue, yellow, red
- Needle hook: 2.5mm

Accessories: Cotton wool, scissors, wool sewing needles

Abbreviated symbols:

MR: magic circle
sl: slip nose
X: single stitch
V: increase nose
A: nose reduction

Making:
I, Head and Body
Row 1. MR, 6X = 6

Row 2. 6V = 12

Row 3. (X, V)*6 = 18

Row 4. (2X,V)*6 = 24

Row 5. (3X,V)*6 = 30

Row 6. (4X,V)*6 = 36

Row 7. (5X,V)*6 = 42

Row 8. (6X,V)*6 =48

Rows 9–15. 48X

Swap pink/blue wool

Row 16. (7X,V)*6 = 54

Rows 17–21. 54X (5 rows)

Row 22. (7X,A)*6 = 48

Row 23. (6X,A)*6 = 42

Row 24. (5X,A)*6 = 36

Row 25. (4X,A)*6 = 30

Row 26. (3X,A)*6 = 24

Row 27. (2X,A)*6 = 18

Row 28. (X,A)*6 = 12

Row 29. 6A = 6

II, Legs (2)

Row 1. MR, 6X = 6

Row 2. 6V = 12

Row 3. (X,A)*4 = 8

Fasten the yarn, leaving a long piece of yarn for sewing

III, Hand (2)

Row 1. MR, 6X = 6

Rows 2–3. 6X = 6

Fasten the yarn, leaving a long piece of yarn for sewing

III, Ears (2)

Row 1. MR, 6X = 6

Row 2. 6X = 6

Row 3. 6V = 12

Row 4. (X, V)*6 = 18

Row 5. (X,A)*6 = 12

Fasten the yarn, leaving a long piece of yarn for sewing

IV, Bow

Row 1. Up 4 pins go back to hook on the 2nd pin: 2X, 4X with the same leg, 2X, 4X with the same leg = 12

Row 2. 2X, (X, V)*2, 2X, (X,V)*2 = 16

Use a long piece of yarn to wrap around the bow. Fasten the yarn, leaving a long piece of yarn to sew the bow on

Finishing products:

+ Sew 2 hands in rows 15-16, about 16 hooks apart

+ Sew 2 legs in rows 19-20-21, about 5 hooks apart

+ Sew the ears at row 9

+ Embroider eyes in rows 10-12, spaced 6 hooks

+ Yellow wool stitch in rows 12-13 between the eyes

+ Embroider mustache with black or brown thread

Tortoise Hook

Materials to prepare:

- Yarn: Wool Jeans Yarn Art Turkey
- Color: blue, brown and beige
- Needle hook: 2.5mm

Accessories: Cotton, woolen needle, scissors, marker

Abbreviated symbols:

sl: slip nose
X: single stitch
V: increase nose
A: nose reduction
BLO- hook on the back thread loop

Making:
I, Blue woolen head
Row 1. MR, 6X = 6

Row 2. 6V= 12

Row 3. (X, V)*6 = 18

Row 4. (2X, V)*6 = 24

Row 5. (3X, V)*6 = 30

Row 6. (4X, V)*6 = 36

Row 7. (5X, V)*6 = 42

Row 8. (6X, V)*6 = 48

Rows 9–17. 48X

Row 18. (6X, A)*6 = 42

Row 19. (5X, A)*6 = 36

Row 20. (4X, A)*6 =30

Row 21. (3X, A)*6 = 24

Row 22. (2X, A)*6 = 18

Attach the eyes, the distance from the eyes to the mouth is 5 hooks

II, Tortoise shell- brown wool

Row 1. MR, 6X = 6

Row 2. 6V= 12

Row 3. (X, V)*6 = 18

Row 4. $(2X, V)^*6 = 24$

Row 5. $(3X, V)^*6 = 30$

Row 6. $(4X, V)^*6 = 36$

Row 7. $(5X, V)^*6 = 42$

Row 8. $(6X, V)^*6 = 48$

Row 9. $(7X, V)^*6 = 54$

Row 10. 54X

Row 11. $(8X, V)^*6 = 60$

Rows 12-17. 60X

Swap beige wool

Row 18. BLO- 60X

Row 19. $(8X, A)^*6 = 54$

Row 20. $(7X, A)^*6 = 48$

Row 21. $(6X, A)^*6 = 42$

Row 22. $(5X, A)^*6 = 36$

Row 23. $(4X, A)^*6 = 30$

Row 24. $(3X, A)^*6 = 24$

Row 25. $(2X, A)^*6 = 18$

Row 26. $(X, A)^*6 = 12$

Hang 27. 6A = 6

III, Forefoot (2)- blue wool
Row 1. MR, 6X = 6
Row 2. 6V= 12
Row 3. (X, V)*6 = 18
Row 4. (2X, V)*6 = 24
Row 5. (3X, V)*6 = 30
Row 6. (4X, V)*6 = 36
Row 7. (5X, V)*6 = 42
X, Double edge, closed 20X hook
Leave a long piece of yarn for sewing
IV, Rear Legs (2)
Row 1. MR, 6X = 6
Row 2. 6V= 12
Row 3. (X, V)*6 = 18
Row 4. (2X, V)*6 = 24
Row 5. (3X, V)*6 = 30
Double edge, closed 14X hook

Finishing products:
+ Sew the head with turtle shell
+ Sew the turtle shell
+ Attach eyes, embroider mouth and cheeks
Good luck!

Colored Octopus Chart

Materials to prepare:

- Wool yarn: Wool Velvet Chopsticks.
- Color: purple, blue, white or pink
- Hook Needle: 10mm

Accessories: Scissors, wool sewing needles, cotton wool, animal eyes.

Abbreviated symbols:

MR: magic circle
X: single stitch
V: increase stitch (2 single stitches on 1 leg)
A: reduce stitches (2 single sts get 1 leg)
sl: slip nose
T: semi-double stitch
F: single double stitch

Making:

I, Head
Row 1. MR, 8X = 8
Row 2. 8V = 16
Row 3. (X, V)*8 = 24
Row 4. (2X, V)*8 = 32
Rows 5-9. 32X
Row 10. (2X, A)*8 = 24
Row 11. FLO- (T, F, T, sl)*12
Fasten yarn, cut wool
II, Lower Body
Row 1. MR, 8X = 8
Row 2. 8V = 16
Row 3. (X, V)*8 = 24
Fasten the yarn, leaving a long piece of yarn for sewing
III, Tentacles (7)
Use colors: white, blue or pink
Row 1. 23 pins

Row 2. Back to hook on 2nd pin: 22V = 44

Fasten the yarn, leaving a long piece of yarn for sewing

IV, Leaf

7 pins return to hook on the 2nd leg: 2F, 1T, X, sl, hook on the opposite side: sl, X, T, 2F, 2 pins, sl

Fasten the yarn, leaving a long piece of yarn for sewing

Finishing products:

+ Stuff the head then sew the bottom body to the head

+ Sew the tentacles

+ Sew leaves on top

Bunny Hook

Materials to prepare:

- Wool yarn: Turkish jeans wool
- Needle hook: 2.5mm

Accessories: accessories: cotton beads, animal eyes, sewing needles, scissors

Symbol:

X: Single nose
V: Rising stitch (2 single sts on the same foot)
A: Reduced sts (2 single stitches together)
W: 3 single sts on the same foot
M: 3 single stitches together

Making:

HEAD

1. 6 X into the magic circle (6)
2. 6 V (12)
3. (1X, V) * 6 (18)
4. (2X, V) * 6 (24)
5. (3X, V) * 6 (30)
6. (4X, V) * 6 (36)
7. (5X, V) * 6 (42)
8. (6X, V) * 6 (48)
9. (7X, V) * 6 (54)
10–15. 54 X (54)
16. 15 X, 8 V, 8 X, 8 V, 15 X. (70)
17–20. 70 X (70)
21. 15 X, 8 A, 8 X, 8 A, 15 X. (54)
22. (7X, A) * 6 (48)
23. (6X, A) * 6 (42)
24. (5X, A) * 6 (36)
25. (4X, A) * 6 (30)
26. (3X, A) * 6 (24)

Leave a piece of excess yarn for sewing. Stuff the head.

FOOT

(Make 2 pieces)
1. 6 X into the magic circle (6) 2. 6 V (12)
3. (1X, V) * 6 (18)
4. 18 X (18)
Cut the wool, leaving a short length of wool and hide the wool. The second leg does not cut the wool, but continues to connect to the body.

DEAR

5. From the 2nd pin, hook 4 pins, 18 X to the first pin, 4 X to one side of the pin, 18 X to the second pin, 4 X to the other side of the pin. (44)
6. (5X, V, 5X) * 4 (48)
7. (7X, V) * 6 (54)

8-17. 54 X (54)
18. (7X, A) * 6 (48)
19-20. 48 X (48)
21. (3X, A, 3X) * 6 (42)
22-23. 42 X (42)
24. (5X, A) * 6 (36)
25. 36 X (36)
26. (4X, A) * 6 (30)
27. 30 X (30)
28. (3X, A) * 6 (24)

HAND

(Make 2 pieces)
1. 6 X into the magic circle
2. 6 DRAW
3-15. 12 XD
16. (1X, A) * 4

EARS

(Make 2 pieces)
1. 6 X into the magic circle
2. 6 DRAW
3. (1X, V) * 6
4-7. 18 XD
8. (1X, A) * 6

CARROT

1. 6 X into the magic circle
2. 6 DRAW
3-4. 12 XD
5. 1 X, A.
6. 9 X, A.
7.8 X, A.
8.7 X, A.
9.6 X, A.
1. 5 X, A. End stitch

LEAVES

MR, (7B, 2V, 4X, slip nose)*3

TOWEL

1. Up to 28 pins, hook on the 4th leg calculate tywf hook needle, 24FV

2. Cluster hook (3B, X)*48

How To Knit A Sweater

1. Materials and tools to prepare

Before learning how to knit a sweater, you need to prepare the following materials and tools:

Knitting rods: 3 pcs

Large yarn wool: 5 - 100 rolls depending on the size of each person's body

1 pair of knitting needles size 7

Tape Ruler: 1 pcs

Sample T-shirt: 1 piece

2. Basic sweater knitting tutorial for beginners

When you have prepared the necessary materials and tools to knit the sweater above.

You can refer to the tutorial on how to knit a sweater for beginners by following the steps below:

2.1 Step 1: Catch the nose and measure
First, when knitting, you make about 15–20 stitches. Do about 10 lines knitting is okay.

Next use a measuring tape to double check the length of each line. You can measure how many stitches or lines 1cm on the ruler corresponds to.

2.2 Step 2: Take body measurements
Use a ruler to measure the width and length of the neck, sleeves, and body of the shirt you're using as a sample.

When you're done measuring, multiply the number of stitches by the size above. Thereby you can calculate the number of stitches you need to knit.

2.3 Step 3: How to crochet a beautiful female sweater on the body

The next step of the beautiful sweater knitting you do is for the body. Using a loop knitting needle, pay attention to catch the correct high line and the number of stitches of the shirt to match the size you have measured on the shirt used as a sample.

Then, continue knitting until the length of the bodice matches the body.

2.4 Step 4: Knit the sleeves

Knitting a beautiful and simple women's shirt, you do the sleeve part by, using a wrist ruler and multiplying by the number of stitches measured in step 1. Then make the correct number of stitches to knit.

In case you prefer to knit loose women's sweaters to make it more comfortable to wear, it is recommended to measure the large arm and take the sleeve measurement.

Continue knitting stitches until the length is full.

Continue knitting the shirt with the same steps for the other arm.

2.5 Step 5: Carry out the hooking part
Knit the hook for the sweater by knitting an extra arm section with a small piece that helps to connect to the armpit.

2.6 Step 6: Connect sleeves and bodice with knitting needles
Remove the sleeve knitting needle gently to avoid slipping the stitches.

Then thread the knitting needles for the sleeves and bodice.

Knit 2 lines of the section above and then mark again.

2.7 Step 7: Knit the neck part

How to knit a beautiful women's sweater next, you proceed to perform the collar. However, you'll need to re-measure the sample shirt first to check your measurements and how many more stitches are needed when making the neckline.

Count the number of stitches on the stick and subtract the number of stitches on the collar. From there you will easily calculate the number of stitches to reduce when knitting the virtual neck.

To reduce the number of stitches needed, you should use 2 pairs of regular sticks.

2.8 Step 8: Finish the shirt

The last step is to complete the knitting, you do the crochet until the right length you want.

You can use a small knitting needle to sew yourself a shirt that fits your body.

How To Knit A Scarf

1. Prepare materials and tools

To make a detailed knitting for a scarf, you need to prepare the following materials and tools:

185m wool (you can choose from many different colors depending on your preference. If you are new to knitting, you should choose a large yarn to make knitting faster)

Large multi-purpose needles: Sizes 8 - 10 (choose large needles if you're new to knitting)

Note: In the framework of this article, Cleanipedia will show you how to change different colors of wool. If you want to knit a scarf in one color, you can skip this technique. And if you want to knit in many colors but do not want to change the type of wool, you can choose a wool roll of different colors.

Regarding knitting needles, if using large knitting needles, the knitting point will be looser than the small knitting needle. So, if you've been knitting hard, you should choose small needles for tighter stitches.

Knitting position: Because knitting time is quite long, so you should keep the sitting position in the chair so that it is most comfortable. Should choose a knitting location that is spacious and has a lot of light to facilitate knitting and movement.

Reference: How to knit a cardigan with 13 easy steps for beginners

2. How to knit a scarf with 10 very simple steps

Here is a simple tutorial on how to knit a scarf you can refer to:

Step 1: First you need to use the color of wool to cause 10-40 stitches, depending on the width of the scarf and the size of the knitting needles.

In case you are just starting to learn knitting, you should choose a small scarf and avoid choosing a scarf that is too large, it will be very time consuming.

If using combed wool and size 8 - 10 knitting needles, you should make 30-40 stitches for the best scarf.

Step 2: Proceed to knit 12 rows with the first wool color.

When performing this step, you should note that you do not have to change the wool to another color and after doing 12 rows of knitting, you may not need to change the color of the wool if you don't want to.

After knitting 12 rows, you can rest your hands at any time. With this knitting style you can do other things flexibly. But it should be noted that knitting enough rows and then stopping, avoid resting your hands while knitting in the middle.

Step 3: Use scissors to cut the yarn when knitting row number 12.

In this step, you should pay attention that after you finish knitting row number 12, you should leave a gap of about 15cm.

You can skip this step if you don't want to change the color of the wool and continue to knit the scarf until you're done. To knit a single-color shawl, you should see the list of dyes on the spool.

Step 4: Change to another wool color.

Continue to make beautiful scarves knitting, you can change to many different colors of wool.

Proceed to tie the excess end of the first wool color to the shorter end of the next wool color. Then, grasp the left hand side and separate it from the long yarn of the skein of yarn to be knitted.

Step 5: Knit the second wool color.

Knit 5 more stitches and stop, then pull the two shorter ends to make it tight.

Step 6: Keep the excess yarn intact.

After you're done knitting, take a crochet needle or a woolen needle to hide it inside the scarf.

Switch to yarn of a different color and avoid cutting excess yarn, as this will reveal difficult-to-repair ties.

Step 7: Knit 12 more rows with new wool color

Do the same knitting as with the first wool color.

Step 8: Add the next wool color (if desired)

For the next step of how to knit a scarf, you can refer to the second knitting color and do the same. Then use scissors to cut the yarn and leave about 15cm of excess.

Repeat this process until you don't want to change the color of the wool. Or you can knit this color more if you want.

Step 9: Knit 12 more rows as color number 2.

Change the color of the wool, with each color you knit 12 rows until you reach the desired length. After knitting, your scarf will have three alternating colors.

Step 10: Extract the knitting stitch.

Finally, you wrap the scarf around your neck and use a crochet needle to mark the excess wool in the scarf.

That's it, you have completed the simple and beautiful way of knitting a scarf. Now is the time for you to experience your results to warm up the winter even more! Good luck!

Knit A Simple Heart-Shaped Scarf

1.1. Knitting materials and tools

To start with this knitting method, you need to prepare yourself a pair of strong knitting needles.

In addition, if knitting men's scarves, you need to prepare 4-5 rolls of wool, and for women's scarves, you only need 2-3 times. You can freely choose the color of wool that you love and combine together to best suit.

1.2. How to knit a scarf with 9 very simple steps

After you have prepared all the necessary materials, let's start learning how to knit heart shapes with Cleanipedia!

Step 1: Make a nose catch

Catching the nose – also known as knitting the thin nose. Determining the number of stitches will depend on how large you want the scarf to be.

If your total number of stitches is odd, the first stitch is only carried over, not knitted. Conversely, if the total number of stitches is even, the stitches at the beginning and end of the row can be knitted or not.

Catch the knitting tip

Normally, we need to knit 28 stitches for the heart-shaped knitting pattern, the first and last stitches are only taken over, not knitted. If you apply this method, the towel will be softer and less wrinkled.

Step 2: Perform spinning

In the first line, do the stitch down and loop 2 loops around the body of the knitting needle.

Step 3: Continue to knit the stitch down

In this step, we continue to knit the stitch down with 2 loops of yarn until the end of the line. Note that when knitting, you should knit loosely, do not knit too tightly so that the wool scarf has just enough softness.

Step 4: Remove and lift the nose of the wool

Take the right black rod and remove and lift the first 2 stitches on the left knitting needle.

Step 5: Change the stitch to the other rod

Gently return the two stitches lifted in step 4 back to the left knitting needle. You should do this step quickly to avoid the stitches from slipping off.

Step 6: Do the down stitch for the 2nd stitch

Perform a down stitch for the inside stitch first, then lift and cross it to the outside stitch. In this step, you should do it very carefully to avoid the case of the wool being stretched too much, making your scarf no longer beautiful.

Step 7: Perform cross stitching of each pair

Similar to step 6, you need to cross-knit each pair until the end of the line. Knit 2 sts first then go back to knit 1 st. Just like that, knitting all the lines you will get the first row of hearts.

Step 8: Repeat from step 2.

Step 9: Perform towel extraction
When the scarf has reached the length you want, you just need to stop knitting and perform the scarf extraction as usual. So finished the super cute heart-shaped scarf.

Crochet A Super Cute Heart Shape

1. Knitting materials and tools

- Wool crochet needle.
- Yarn, cotton wool or parasol yarn.
- Some decorative materials are optional.

Needles are only used for sewing wool in case you do not know how to assemble wool with crochet needles.

Cotton for stuffing and wire hangers for decoration.

2. How to knit a heart shape with 7 easy steps

Step 1: First of all, you need to do 8 stitches of chain crochet, then turn the crochet needle back to the row of 7 single stitches (not counting the stitch close to the needle), so that you can crochet the entire row with a single stitch.

Step 2: Continuously alternate crocheting a total of 8 single stitches as above on both sides of the product until a square piece of wool is obtained.

This piece of wool will be the center of the heart that you need to crochet. Hook two more curved stitches at the top to make the heart shape easier.

On each side of the heart stitch will be crocheted with a seashell stitch – consisting of many double stitches with the same foot – just follow these steps

Sequentially: choose a stitch right in the middle of the square edge of the piece of wool to make the base of the nose,

Then then knit 7 double double crochet stitches; Do the same right on the next square edge, finally ending with a move to lock the row of wool.

Step 3: To knit a larger heart shape as you want, need to crochet an extra row of double stitches around it.

Make 3 chain stitches first with the same length as a double crochet stitch, then knit another 6 double crochet stitches until the stock is gone.

Step 4: When knitting to the point of the heart shape, you make 3 double stitches with the same nose to make the wool have more spread. Then knit 7 double stitches in a row. Go to the bend of the heart, knit 2 double stitches on the same leg and repeat 6 times.

The next stitch is to do a low double crochet, go to the center of the two halves of the heart as a single stitch, then continue to crochet symmetrically in sequence: 1 low double, then 2 double doubles on the same leg, and repeat. 6 times again. Finally, knit one more stitch to join the rows of yarn, knot and remove excess yarn.

Step 5: After performing the above steps, you have completed one side of the heart.

You just need to knit one more piece like that, then use a knitting needle or crochet needle to knit a single crochet stitch that connects the edges of the 2 heart pieces together.

When the crochet is almost done, don't finish it quickly, leave a small hole and stuff it inside until it's full, then continue crocheting to the end.

Step 6: To make the products look more lovely and eye-catching, decorate them with button beads, small bells or accessories.

Step 7: Work hard to do this heart-shaped knitting every day. Once you get used to it, you can freely create countless different lovely heart hooks. This is sure to be a lovely little gift.

How To Knit A Beanie

1. Prepare materials and tools

- 100g organic cotton Etrofil wool
- 6mm - 15mm . circular knitting needles
- Tape measure
- Drag
- Straight knitting needles

Pro tip: The easiest way to knit a beanie is to use thick wool to make crochet faster. The thicker the wool, the softer and warmer the hat will be.

2. How to knit a beanie very simple with 7 steps

Before starting this detailed knitting, you should find out first what is the difference between the forward stitch and the crochet stitch.

2.1 Taking measurements and sketching drawings

Before you start, you'll need to take your head measurements to measure how many stitches will fit the circumference of your head or that of the person you're giving it to.

Using yarn and knitting needles, you knit 10 stitches and smooth 10 rows to create a small square pattern.

Here, smooth knitting is knitting the right side down, then the left side knitting the nose up. Be careful not to pull too hard on the yarn.

Set the ruler to measure the width and the width of the knitting pattern. With this method, you will find out how many stitches 1cm corresponds to.

Divide the number of stitches by the length of the pattern. For example, if the sample measures 14cm long, you divide 10 stitches by 14cm, the result is 0.71 stitches per 1cm.

Measure the circumference of your head using the formula to subtract 10cm from the index to make sure the hat fits snugly on the head. Assuming the head is 58cm – 58cm, subtract 10cm and you will get the number 48cm.

Next, you calculate how many stitches 48cm will be. When you search for the keyword how to knit a simple beanie, you will find that there are many different conversion formulas.

The easiest calculation that Cleanipedia wants to reveal to you is to multiply the circumference by the product of the stitches calculated above, which means 48cm x 0.71 = 34cm. This number means you need 34 stitches to achieve a circumference of 48cm.

This method has the advantage that it is not too difficult to perform and ensures the right size of the beanie after completion.

2.2 Starting to thin the nose

After the warm-up, it's time to start learning how to knit a real beanie. In this step, you will knit the calculated number of stitches and add a circular stitch. First, you tie the two ends of the yarn together, holding the left hand side. The right hand uses the rod to pierce the loop of wool and take the stick as the center. You will see the yarn on top and the yarn on the bottom. With your left hand raised, use your index finger to loop it around to hold the top yarn. Particularly, the thumb holds the yarn under.

Then, you stick the stick from the bottom up into the loop of wool at the thumb. Pull through the loop of yarn on your index finger from top to bottom. Thread through the loop of yarn at the thumb, keeping the stitch just above the rod. Gently pull your thumb out of the loop. Use your index finger to squeeze the last stitch into the rod body. Repeat these steps on the next stitch until the row is gone.

2.3 Knitting circles

After the stitch step, you will move on to knitting circles. When you first learn how to knit a beanie, this step will be a little difficult for you, but just follow the video tutorial below.

Transfer the pattern with the excess stitch on the back needle to the front needle. Place the yarn you are knitting on the needle first to knit the stitch up and down.

To join the top and bottom of the pattern, pull the back needle forward and pass it between the first two stitches of the previous needle.

2.4 Knitting hat brim

The brim of the beanie will be made up of 3 rows of knitting and knitting up and down. In the top row, keep the yarn as taut as possible.

This will help keep the brim tight and comfortable. First, knit a complete row. Move to the end of the needle, rotate the fabric pattern and thread it through the needle first. Use the back needle to knit the second stitch. Next, knit down in the second row, knit up in the third and last row.

2.5 Knit the body of the hat

After knitting the hat brim, you will start knitting the body of the hat. The body will only use the stitch to knit down. As you knit the top 3 rows, slowly reduce the tension on the yarn you are knitting to gradually transition from the hem to the main body.

After knitting the first 3 rows, you continue to knit down and still keep the tension on the yarn you are knitting. This way of knitting the beanie will help the body hat look soft when finished. Continue knitting until the hat body reaches 20cm. You can adjust the size depending on the head circumference.

2.6 Knitting hats

When knitting the hat body reaches the desired size, you move to the step of knitting the hat. To do this step, you will reduce the number of stitches so that the rows narrow. Similar to the body, you only use the down stitch technique.

In the first hat row, knit the first and second stitches together. Begin knitting two normal crochet stitches. Repeat until the last row. The next row is the "break row" where you will knit all the stitches normally. In the second and last row, you knit the two stitches together and finish with a normal stitch. In the video tutorial there are a total of 16 stitches on the needle.

2.7 Finishing

To complete the beanie, you proceed to cut the yarn you are doing, leaving the remaining length about 30cm.

Thread the yarn you are knitting onto the weft knitting needle. Next, using a weft, thread the yarn through each stitch in the last row. Once done, repeat one more stitch. Stretch until the hole of the hat is completely closed.

Use the crosshair to hide the yarn on the inside of the hat. Cut off the excess wool. Finally, hide the top yarn by threading it through nearby stitches. At the end of this step, your beanie is done

Knit A Wool Bag

1. Prepare materials and tools

Before starting the process of creating your own wool bag, prepare all the materials and tools you need when knitting a beautiful scarf pattern, or a beautiful sweater pattern. This will make your next steps easier.

The things you need to prepare to do the detailed knitting are as follows:
Yarn (choose your favorite color)
Knitting needles: it doesn't matter what size but Cleanipedia recommends 5.00mm (US 8)
Scissors (preferably sewing scissors, or regular scissors that can cut the yarn easily)
A sewing needle + a button
Thread (choose a color that matches the yarn color to create a nice uniformity)

A little patience from you as this may take more than 3 hours to complete.

2. Knitting

Once everything is ready, let's get to work! First, cast on 20 seams to make sure for the next steps.

3. Knit in rows

This is the next step in how to knit a simple and easy bag. Let's continue to make a row of knitting from the 20 ready-made stitches in the previous step, not too difficult right?

4. Finish the bag side

Once you've completed the first row, repeat that knitting step to create the next rows. It is estimated that you should knit about 84 more times to create the right size for the lovely wool bag.

5. Sew the rows back

When we have finished creating the knitting step, we will stitch the stitches together and leave one last stitch for the next step.

6. Finish stitching the rows

Next you will put the loops over each other, then you will gently pull the end over the loop you just created and then tighten.

7. Knit the bottom of the bag

Add this step and you're halfway through the knitting process. Next you just need to knit the bottom of the two sides of the bag together so that they form the bottom for the wool bag. A small note is to knit carefully to ensure your certainty.

8. Knit the sides of the bag

In this step, fold a piece of the bag off to one side to form a square with a flap of about 5cm. Next, you knit the sides together to form the complete bag.

9. Button stitch

After completing the main part, it will be time to make the extra parts to make your bag "perfect".

Take your favorite button and sew it in the center of the front and just below the flap of the bag.

10. Create a ring
This is quite a difficult step, but don't worry because with a simple knitting bag you will do it right away. Once you've finished sewing the knot, cut a 20cm piece of yarn. Next, tie the yarn on the top center flap. At this point, you should double knot. Finally, you loop the yarn around the knot and tie it in the same position as the other knot.

11. Make a bracelet
A bracelet for a wool bag will help you transform many different styles. To complete this step, first cut 3 pieces of yarn the same size. You can then make the handle larger or smaller depending on your size. Finally, braid the 3 parts together and knot both ends. Simple isn't it?

12. Knit wrist strap and bag

After completing the bracelet, we will connect the bracelet to the bag to make it more perfect. First, take the needle and thread and then place the tip of your handle on the bag. It is recommended to place the top right along the seam to make it easier. Next, secure your handle to the bag. Do the same with the left side.

13. Finished Product

And after a series of steps mentioned above, you have the finished product, isn't it amazing?

Deer Tote Bag

Materials to prepare:

Wool yarn: YarnArt Jeans wool imported from
Turkey
Color: pink, white, …
Needle hook: number 2.5mm
Accessories: wool sewing needles, wool cutting
scissors, ...

Sign

MR: magic circle
X: single stitch
V: increase the nose (2 stitches on 1 leg)
A: reduce the stitches (2 stitches together)
How to make: (13 - 15cm)

Learn how to pickpocket a deer
A – Bag

I, Bottom of the bag

Hook 25 chain hooks
1. 1V, 22X, 4X, 22X, 1V . end stitch

2. 2V, 22X, 4V, 22X, 2V

3. 1X, 1V, 26X, 1V, 2X, 1V, 26X, 1V, X

II, Body bag

Crochet half double nose according to each person's length
B – Tai
I, Big ears

H1: double 9 stitch magic circle
H2 (2 double sts with the same foot) 4 times, 1 double + 2 doubles + 1 double with the same foot, (2 times with the same foot) 4 times

II, Small Ears

H1 magic circle, 7 double stitches

H2 (2 sts with the same foot) 3 times, 1 double + 2 doubles + 1 double with the same foot, (2 sts with the same foot) 3 times
C – White nose part

Hook 1 chain consisting of 16 chain hooks, onto 1 pin and reduce the stitches at both ends to form an r. Finish sticking to the bag with candle glue

D – Flower
Hook 21 pins, hook 2 with the same foot on the 4th leg, on 3 hooks, move the nose to the next leg

Up 3 crochet hooks 2 double the same foot to the next leg, up 3 crochet hooks move to the next leg, keep crocheting until the end of the row

Crochet Brown Mouse Chart Template

Materials to prepare:

- Yarn: Turkish YarnArt Jeans Wool
- Color: dark beige (A), dark blue (B), white (C), black (D)
- Needle hook: 2.5mm
- Accessories: Cotton wool, scissors, wool sewing needles

Abbreviated symbols:

MR: magic circle
X: single stitch
V: increase nose
A: nose reduction
F: single double stitch
T: semi-double stitch
BLO- hook on the back loop of wool
FLO- crochet on front wool loop
Sl: slip nose

Making:

I, Body
Start with color A
Row 1. MR, 7X = 7
Row 2. 7V = 14
Row 3. (X,V)*7 = 21
Row 4. (2X,V)*7 = 28
Row 5. (3X,V)*7 = 35
Row 6. (4X,V)*7 = 42
Row 7. BLO- 42X
Rows 8-9. 42X
Row 10. (4X,V)*6 = 48
Rows 11-12. 48X
Change wool color BLUE
Rows 13-14. 48X
Row 15. 13X, (A, 2X)*5, A, 13X = 42
Rows 16-17. 42X
Change wool color
Row 18. (5X,A)*6 = 36
Row 19-20. 36X

Change wool color BLUE

Row 21. 36X

Change wool color A

Row 22. BLO-36X

Row 23. (4X,A)*6 = 30

Row 24-25. 30X

Start stuffing

Row 26. (8X,A)*3 = 27

Row 27. 27X

Row 28. (7X,A)*3 = 24

Row 29. 24X

Row 30. (2X,A)*6 = 18

Row 31. (X,A)*6 = 12

Row 32.6A= 6

Collar hook: at 22nd row, attach blue yarn FLO crochet: onto 2 pieces, crochet 1 F stitch for each leg until the end of the row, sl. Cut wool

II, Muzzle

Start coloring EASY

Row 1. MR, 6X = 6

Row 2. 6X

Change wool color A

Row 3. (X, V)*3 = 9

Row 4. (2X, V)*3 = 12

Rows 5-6. 12X

Row 7. 3T, X = 4

Pin the yarn, leaving a long piece of yarn for sewing. Sew the muzzle to rows 22-27

III, Ears (2)

Row 1. MR, 6X = 6

Row 2. 6V = 12

Row 3. (X,V)*7 = 21

Row 4. (2X,V)*7 = 28

Row 5. (3X,V)*7 = 35

Row 6. (4X,V)*7 = 42

Pin the yarn, leaving a long piece of yarn for sewing. Use black thread to embroider the eyes on row 25

IV, Legs (2)

Row 1. MR, 6X = 6

Row 2. 6V = 12

Rows 3–7. 12X

Stuffed

Row 8. (2X, A)*3 = 9

Row 9. Fold the legs and hook 4X to close the legs

Fasten the yarn, leaving a long piece of yarn for sewing

V, Tail (wool A)

Up to 21 pins, go back to hook on the 2nd leg: 20sl

VI, Hand (2)

Start wool color A

Row 1. MR, 6X = 6

Row 2. (V, V)*3 = 9

Row 3. 9X

Change wool color BLUE

Rows 4–8. 9X

Change wool color

Rows 9–10. 9X

Row 11. Fold your legs and hook 4X to close your hands

Pin the yarn, leaving a long piece of yarn for sewing. Hand sewn at rows 18-20

Cut 3 strands of color A wool about 5cm long, then use a crochet needle to attach it to the head to make the hair

Finishing products:

You stuffed and sewed as follows:

+ Sew the muzzle to the row 22-27

+ Sew 2 hands and 2 legs

+ Sew the ears on the head

+ Sew the tail at the back

Crop Top Wool Crochet Chart

Materials to prepare:

- Wool yarn: Anne yarn or can be substituted with Lace . yarn
- Needle: No. 1.75
- Accessories: wool sewing needles, scissors.

Making:

Step 1: Create a magic circle, hook in turn in order: 4 double, 2 pin, 4 double, 2 pin, 4 double, 2 pin, 4 double, 2 pin.

Beautiful wool croptop crochet chart for you to go to the beach
Finish round 1 with a slip stitch.

Round 2: Up 3 pins, crochet 4 double stitches (each double stitch is hooked to 1 leg), 2 double 2 pins 2 double into the hole in the middle of the right corner. Repeat until the end of the round.

You crochet 9 loops. Pin the nose and cut the yarn.

Step 2: Take turns crocheting the same 8 squares as above

Step 3: Use a sewing needle to sew them together

Beautiful wool croptop crochet chart for you to go to the beach
You should note that the stitches are clever and the stitches correspond to each other, so that at the end of the row, the 2 squares are misaligned.

Step 4: After completing the stitching of the square panels together, you crochet 5 double crochet stitches to the top of 1 square. Repeat these 5 double crochet stitches until the strap is 20cm long.
Securely sew the strap with the square tip on the back

Step 5: Decorate the crop top with tassels.

Red Radish Chart Hook

Materials to prepare:

- Wool yarn: Turkish YarnArt Jeans Wool, Milk Cotton 125gr.
- Color: red, white and blue.
- Hook needle: 2.5mm.
- Accessories: Cotton wool, scissors, wool sewing needles.

Abbreviated symbols:

MR: magic circle
X: single stitch
V: increase stitch (2 single stitches on 1 leg)
A: reduce stitches (2 single sts get 1 leg)
T: semi-double stitch
sl: slip nose
F: single double stitch

Making:
I, Radish stem

Start wool red
Row 1. MR, 6X = 6
Row 2. 6V = 12
Row 3. (X, V)*6 = 18
Row 4. (2X, V)*6 = 24
Row 5. (3X, V)*6 = 30
Rows 6-9. 30X
Row 10. (3X, A)*6 = 24
Row 11. 24X
Swap white wool
Row 12. (3X, A)*5 = 20
Row 13. (2X, A)*5 = 15
Stuff and crochet again
Row 14. (2X, A)*4 = 12
Row 15. 6A = 6
Hook up 12 pins, thread dowel to cut yarn

II, Leaves – green

Up 20 pins go back to hook on the 2nd leg: X, T, 6F, 1T, 3X with the same foot, continue to hook: 1T, 6F, 1T, 1X, sl. Do not cut the wool, but slide the tip into the middle of the leaf to hook the veins.
Then on a piece of twine, dowel and cut the yarn
The second card is similarly hooked up to about 25 cards
3rd card up to 30 cards
4th card to 15 cards

Finishing products:
Remember to leave a long piece of yarn to sew on the radish!

Chart Fluffy Wool Hats

Materials to prepare:

- Yarn Yarn: Turkish Art Yarn Jeans, Fluffy Up
- Color: white, brown
- Needle hook: 2.5mm
- Accessories: scissors, sewing needles

Abbreviated symbols:
X: single stitch
V: increase nose
A: nose reduction

Making:

Row 1: MR, 11X = 11
Row 2: 11V = 22
Row 3. XV*11= 33
Row 4. 2XV*11= 44
Row 5. 3XV*11= 55
Row . 4XV*11= 66
Row 7.5. 5XV*11= 77

Row 8. 6XV*11= 88
Row 9. 88X
Row 10. 7XV*11
Row 11. 8XV*11
Row 12. 9XV*11

The next rows crochet all the X stitches until you have the desired length of the hood

Covered ears
After crocheting the hat, continue to crochet 11 stitches X
Row 1. 1 return pin: A, 7X, A
Row 2. 1 return pin: 9X
Row 3. 1 pin returns: A, 5X, A
Row 4. 1 return pin: 7X
Row 5. 1 return pin: A, 3X, A
Row 6. 1 pin returns: A, A, A
Row 7. 1 pin, 2A
Do the same for the rest of the ear cups. Make the 2 sides equal

After crocheting the ear flaps, add 1 more row of
Xs around the hat and 2 hooded ears

Lanyard part

Row 1. MR, 6X = 6

Row 2. 6V = 12

Row 3. (XV)*6= 18

Rows 4-6. 18X = 18

Row 7. (XA)*6 = 12

Row 8.6. 6A= 6

Finishing products:

Stuffed. Hook 30 sts then connect to the ear hood
and hook 30X back. Sew tight to the circle

Do the same in the other ear. So complete the
baby boy's beanie

Hook Uncle Hippo

Materials to prepare:

- Yarn: Wool Jeans Yarn Art Turkey
- Color: wool beige, blue
- Needle hook: 2.5mm
- Accessories: Cotton, sewing needles, scissors, marker, black plastic eye

Abbreviated symbols:

X: single stitch
V: increase nose
A: nose reduction
Sl: slip nose
T: semi-double stitch
BLO- crochet on the back half of the wool loop
Making:
I, Head
Row 1. MR, 6X = 6
Row 2. 6V = 12

Row 3. (V,X)*6 = 18
Row 4. (V,2X)*6 = 24
Row 5. (V,3X)*6 = 30
Row 6. (V,4X)*6 = 36
Rows 7-10. 36X
Row 11. (A, 4X)*6 = 30
Row 12. (A, 3X)*6 = 24
Row 13. (A, 2X)*6 = 18
Row 14. 18X
Row 15. (V, 2X)*6 = 24
Row 16. (V, 3X)*6 = 30
Rows 17-20. 30X
Row 21. (A,3X)*6 = 24
Row 22. (A, 2X)*6 = 18
Row 23. (A, X)*6 = 12
Stuffed
Row 24. 6A= 6
Fasten yarn, cut wool
II, Ear (2)
MR, 8 billion

III, Nose (2)

Row 1. Up to 4 balls
Row 2. Return hook to the 2nd pin on the left of the needle: 2X, sl. Fasten the yarn, leaving a long piece of yarn for sewing
IV, Legs (4)
Row 1. MR, 6X = 6
Row 2. 6V = 12
Item 3.Blo- 12X
Rows 4-5. 12X
Row 6. (A, 4X)*2= 10
Fasten the yarn, leaving a long piece of yarn for sewing
V, Than
Row 1. MR, 6X = 6
Row 2. 6V = 12
Row 3. (V,X)*6 = 18
Row 4. (V,2X)*6 = 24
Row 5. (V,3X)*6 = 30

Row 6. (V,4X)*6 = 36

Rows 7-17. 36X

Row 18. (A,4X)*6 = 30

Row 19. (A,3X)*6 = 24

Row 20. (A,2X)*6 = 18

Row 21. (A, X)*6 = 12

Fasten the yarn, leaving a long piece of yarn for sewing

Finishing products:

+ Attach the plastic eye on the head

+ Sew 2 ears to the head 4 rows from the eyes, 2 ears separated by 6 hooks

+ Stitch stitches at cave 6, 2 stitches are about 4-5 hooks apart

+ Sew the body with the head

+ Sew 4 legs below the body

+ Attach the hook needle to the back of the body, pick up 7 pins and return to the hook: (2X with the same leg)* to the end to form the tail

+ Use blue wool to crochet a long string to make a bow tie. Fasten yarn, cut wool

Shoe Hook

Materials to prepare:

- Wool yarn: YarnArt Jeans wool imported from Turkey
- Color: original chart blue, gray. You can choose the color of wool as you like
- Needle hook: number 2.5mm

Accessories: sewing needles, wool scissors, 2 buttons
Sign

Rnd: Goods
X: single stitch
T: semi-double sts, VT: increments of semi-double sts
F: single double stitch

How to make shoes

Sample hook for 10 stitches and 10 rows, measure 5x5cm or 2x2in, use 3.25 crochet needle or size to fit baby's feet

Please use a semi-double stitch to crochet

Rnd 1: 11[13,14] pin, return hook on 3rd leg: 1T, 7T[9,10], 6T with same leg, opposite side hook, 7T[9,10], 5T with same leg, slip nose .

Rnd 2: 1 pin, 8T[10,11], 5VT, 8T[10,11], 5VT, nose slip.

Rnd 3: 1 pin, 8T[10,11], (1VT, 1T)*5, 8T[10,11], (1Vt, 1T)*5, nose slip.

Above:

Rnd 1: 1 pin, (BLO) (46X [50 52]), nose slip.

Rnd 2: 1 pin, (46X[50,52]), missed nose.
Rnd 3-4: repeat Rnd2

Right shoe strap:

Without cutting, continue crocheting 16 [17,18] pins, return to the 7th foot, 1F each, slide the toe, continue to crochet 15F on the back of the shoe. Yarn dowel

Left shoelace: Thread, hook symmetrically with the right shoe 16[17,18] pin, return to hook on the 7th foot 1F each, slide the toe, continue to crochet 15F on the back of the shoe. Yarn dowel

Flower:

Use the color of your choice

On 4 pins, slide the stitch into a circle

Rnd 1: 1 pin, 9X into the circle, slide the nose

Rnd 2: (5 pins, 1X)*8

Rnd 3: 3X in the 1st petal, then you put the flower on the front of the shoe and slide the toe onto the 4th crochet foot [6, 7] from the last single double toe for the right shoelace (or on the right foot). 4th hook [6, 7] from the base of the left second). 3X in the same wing, (3X in the next wing, skip the 3 hook pins, slide the nose into the next hook foot, 3X in the same wing)*5, (3X in the next wing, 1 pin, 3X in the same 1 wings)* repeat 1 more time, slide the nose. Yarn dowel

Perfect product
You have just finished the shoe pattern for your baby, then sew the button on the shoelaces

Crochet Teddy Basket Pattern

Materials to prepare:

- Wool yarn: Plain Yarn, Plain Yarn, Simply, Ribbon
- Color: beige, light gray (color depends on preference)
- Hook Needle: 3-3.5mm
- Accessories: Crochet needles, scissors, markers, wool sewing needles

Abbreviated symbols:

X: single stitch
V: increase nose
A: nose reduction
Sl: slip nose
Making:
I, Than
Row 1. MR, 6X = 6
Row 2. 6V = 12

Row 3. $(X,V)^\star 6 = 18$
Row 4. $(X, V, X)^\star 6 = 24$
Row 5. $(3X, V)^\star 6 = 30$
Row 6. $(2X, V, 2X)^\star 6 = 36$
Row 7. $(5X, V)^\star 6 = 42$
Row 8. $(3X, V, 3X)^\star 6 = 48$
Row 9. $(7X, V)^\star 6 = 54$
Row 10. $(4X, V, 4X)^\star 6 = 60$
Row 11. $(9X, V)^\star 6 = 66$
Row 12. $(5X, V, 5X)^\star 6 = 72$
Row 13. $(11X, V)^\star 6 = 78$
Row 14. $(6X, V, 6X)^\star 6 = 84$
Row 15. $(13X, V)^\star 6 = 90$
Row 16. $(7X, V, 7X)^\star 6 = 96$
Row 17. $(15X, V)^\star 6 = 102$
Rows 18–49. 102X

II, Bear Ears (2)

Row 1. MR, $6X = 6$

Row 2. 6V = 12
Row 3. (X,V)*6 = 18
Row 4. (2X, V)*6 = 24
Rows 5-8. 24X
Row 9. (2X, A)*6 = 18
Row 10. (X, A)*6 = 12
Fasten the yarn, leaving a long piece of yarn for sewing

III, Bear Mouth
Row 1. MR, 6X = 6
Row 2. 6V = 12
Row 3. (X,V)*6 = 18
Row 4. (2X, V)*6 = 24
Row 5. (3X, V)*6 = 30
Row 6. (2X, V, 2X)*6 = 36
Row 7. (5X, V)*6 = 42
Row 8. 42X
Fasten the yarn, leaving a long piece of yarn for sewing

IV, Bear Nose

Up 5 pins, go back to hook on the 2nd leg: V, 2X, W, 2X, V = 11

Fasten the yarn, leaving a long piece of yarn for sewing

Finishing products:

Sewing bear ears

Attach eyes

Sew mouth and nose

Chart Hook Flower Watering Pot

Materials to prepare:

- Wool yarn: Turkish YarnArt Jeans Wool, Milk Cotton 125g.
- Color: blue, yellow or your favorite color.
- Needle hook: 2.5mm
- Accessories: Scissors, sewing needles, cotton wool, plastic eyes,

Abbreviated symbols:

MR: magic circle
X: single stitch
V: increase stitch (2 single stitches on 1 leg)
A: reduce stitches (2 single sts get 1 leg)
F: single double stitch
SL: Slip nose
T: semi-double stitch

Making:

I, Body

Row 1. MR, 6X = 6

Row 2. 6V = 12

Row 3. (X, V)*6 = 18

Row 4. (2X, V)*6 = 24

Row 5. (3X, V)*6 = 30

Row 6. (4X, V)*6 = 36

Row 7. (5X, V)*6 = 42

Row 8. (6X, V)*6 = 48

Row 9. BLO- 48X

Row 10-11. 48X

Row 12. (6X, A)*6 = 42

Rows 13-16. 42X

Row 17. (5X, A)*6 = 36

Rows 18-21. 36X

Row 22. (4X,A)*6 = 30

Row 23. BLO- 30X

Row 24. (3X, A)*6 = 24

Row 25. 24X

Row 26. (2X, A)*6 = 18
Row 27. (X, A)*6 = 12
Row 28. 6A = 6
Cut wool
II, Faucet and rose
Start with white wool
Row 1. MR, 6X = 6
Row 2. 6V = 12
Row 3. (X, V)*6 = 18
Row 4. 18X
Change to blue
Rows 5-6. 18X
Row 7. (X,A)*6 = 12
Rows 8-11. 12X
Row 12. V, 11X = 13
Rows 13-16. 13X
Row 17. V, 5X, 4sl, 2X, 4F, 1X, sl
Fasten the yarn, leaving a long piece of yarn for sewing
III, flower

Row 1. 3 pins return to hook on the 3rd leg: 1F, 2 pins, sl

Row 2. 2 pins in the middle, 1F, 2 pins, sl

Row 3. 2 pins, 1F, 2 pins, sl

Fasten yarn, cut wool

Crochet 4 pink and 4 white flowers

IV, Leaf

4 pins return to hook on the 2nd pin on the left side of the needle: X, 1T, sl

Fasten the yarn, leaving a long piece of yarn for sewing

Hook about 5-8 leaves

V, Top handle

Row 1. 22 balls

Row 2 - 3. 22X

Fasten the yarn, leaving a long piece of yarn for sewing

VI, Bottom Handle

Row 1. MR, 5X

Rows 2-19. 5X

Fasten the yarn, leaving a long piece of yarn for sewing

VII, Cheek (2)

MR, 6X = 6

Finishing products:

You stuffed and sewed the parts

+ Sewing warm faucet

+ Sew 2 parts of the straps to the kettle

+ Sew flowers on top

+ Attach the eyes, sew the cheeks and use black thread to embroider the nose

Dinosaur Rattle Hook

Materials to prepare:

- Wool yarn: Turkish YarnArt Jeans wool
- Color: pink, cream white
- Needle hook: 2.5mm
- Accessories: woolen scissors, woolen sewing needles, 12mm animal eyes, 7cm round rattles

Abbreviated symbols:

MR: Magic circle
X: Single crochet stitch
V: Increase the nose (2 stitches on 1 leg)
A: Stitch reduction (2 crochet stitches)
B: Sprocket/chain tip

Making:

I. Dinosaur rattle head (Pink)
H1. MR, 6X (6)
H2. 6V (12)

H3. (X, V)*6 (18)
H4. (2X, V)*6 (24)
H5. (3X, V)*6 (30)
H6. (4X, V)*6 (36)
H7. (5X, V)*6 (42)
H8. (6X, V)*6 (48)
H9-H13. 48X (48)
H14. (6X, A)*6 (42)
H15-H16. 42X (42)
H17. (5X, A)*6 (36)
H18-H19. 36X (36)
H20. (4X, A)*6 (30)
H21-H22. 30X(30)
H23. (3X, A)*6 (24)
H24-H25. 24X (24)
H26. (2X, A)*6 (18)
H27-H28. (X, A)*6 (12)
H28. 6A (6)

II. Dinosaur rattle tail (Pink)

H1. MR, 6X (6)

H2. (2X, V)*2 (8)

H3. (3X, V)*2 (10)

H4. (X, V, 3X)*2 (12)

H5. (5X, V)*2 (14)

H6. A, 5X, V, 6X (14)

H7. (2X, V, 4X)*2 (16)

H8. (A, 7X, V, 6X (16)

H9. (7X, V)*2 (18)

H10. (5X, V)*3 (21)

H11. 6X, V, 6X, V, 5X, A (22)

H12. A, 7X, V, 4X, V, 7X (23)

H13. 11X, V, 11X (24)

H14. (7X, V)*3(27)

H15. X, A, 12X, V, 11X (27)

H16. 10X, V, 6X, V, 9X (29)

H17. X, A, 8X, V, 8X, V, 8X (30)

H18. (9X, V)*3 (33)

H19. 6X, V, (4X, V)*4, 6X (38)

III. Dinosaur eyes inside (White)

H1. MR, 6X (6)

H2. 6V (12)

H3. (X, V) *6 (18)

H4. 18X (18)

H5. (X, A)*6 (12)

IV. Outer Dinosaur Eye (Pink)

H1. Initialize 4B

H2. X, V, X

H3. X,V, 2X

H4. V, X, V, X, V (8)

H5. 3X, V, 3XV

H6. 4X, V, 4X, DRAW

H7. 5X, V, 5X, DRAW

IV. Horn (Pink)

H1. MR, 6X (6)

H2. 6V (12)

H3-H5. 12X (12)

Finishing products:

Printed in Great Britain
by Amazon

40384101R00086